TINY THINGS, BIG IMPACTS

SPIDERS

Written by John Wood

KidHaven PUBLISHING

Published in 2020 by
KidHaven Publishing, an Imprint of Greenhaven Publishing, LLC
353 3rd Avenue
Suite 255
New York, NY 10010

This edition is published by arrangement with Booklife Publishing

Edited by: Kirsty Holmes
Designed by: Jasmine Pointer

Cataloging-in-Publication Data

Names: Wood, John.
Title: Spiders / John Wood.
Description: New York : KidHaven Publishing, 2020. | Series: Tiny things, big impacts | Includes glossary and index.
Identifiers: ISBN 9781534532892 (pbk.) | ISBN 9781534532915 (library bound) | ISBN 9781534532908 (6 pack) | ISBN 9781534532922 (ebook)
Subjects: LCSH: Spiders--Juvenile literature.
Classification: LCC QL458.4 W663 2020 | DDC 595.4'4--dc23

Printed in the United States of America

CPSIA compliance information: Batch #BW20KL: For further information contact Greenhaven Publishing LLC, New York, New York at 1-844-317-7404.

Please visit our website, www.greenhavenpublishing.com. For a free color catalog of all our high-quality books, call toll free 1-844-317-7404 or fax 1-844-317-7405.

PHOTO CREDITS

All images are courtesy of Shutterstock.com, unless stated otherwise.

Cover – iSKYDANCER, www.hollandfoto.net. 4 – Gluiki, sydeen, Iskydancer. 5 – cpaulfell, Nancy Tripp Photography. 6 – Rdguy, Peter Waters. 7 – amirhamzaa, dmitriyGo. 8 – kosmos111, pukach, Akin_EO. 9 – Cathy Keifer. 10 – Angel_AMX, Ruslan Ivantsov, Nyvlt-art. 11 – Jiri Hera, AZP Worldwide. 12 – Alexey Boldin, sakhorn. 13 – Eric Buermeyer, Coprid. 14 – photastic, Rawpixel.com, GreenLandStudio. 15 – nechaevkon, zaidi razak. 16 – reddees, sraphotohut, Katarina Christenson, SLdesign. 17 – Paul Looyen, napocska. 18 – Nadezda Murmakova, vladibulgakov, Paladin12. 19 – Ian Fletcher, YuRi Photolife. 20 – Palau, Abd. Halim Hadi, Jarun Tedjaem. 21 – Artsiom Petrushenka, Vetlas. 22 – D. Kucharski K. Kucharska, SFIO CRACHO, moj0j0, TopVectorElements, Maquiladora, Rvector. 23 – Eric Isselee, Chinch, Maquiladora, VectorShow, A7880S, wectors, AlexHliv, robuart. 24 – Dominator, Petr Klabal. 25 – Protasov AN, vladimir salman. 26 – cornfield, Fabio Lamanna. 27 – BABAROGA, Rich Carey. 28 – BEJITA, Mary Terriberry. 29 – Gavin Baker Photography, Uditha Wickramanayaka. 30 – Petra Eisenbart, visdia.

SPIDERS

CONTENTS:

WORDS THAT LOOK LIKE THIS ARE EXPLAINED IN THE GLOSSARY ON PAGE 31.

MEET THE SPIDER

This is a spider. Like other bugs, spiders are much smaller than us. However, unlike some other bugs, spiders change the world every day. They might seem unimportant, but without them our lives would be very different indeed.

Spider Sizes

Spiders are a very **diverse** group of creatures. In some places in the world, most spiders are small and won't hurt you. In other places, like Australia, spiders can be very big and dangerous.

Giant Huntsman Spider

THE GIANT HUNTSMAN HAS THE BIGGEST LEG SPAN – IT IS 12 INCHES (30 CM) ACROSS!

THE SAMOAN MOSS SPIDER IS ONE OF THE SMALLEST, AND IS ONLY 0.3 MILLIMETER ACROSS.

Silk

Every spider is able to make a material called silk. Spiders have **glands** inside their bodies that create the silk. The spider pulls the silk out of its body through body parts called spinnerets.

SPIDER SILK IS TOUGHER THAN STEEL. IT MIGHT NOT SEEM LIKE IT BECAUSE SPIDERS SPIN A SMALL, THIN AMOUNT TO MAKE THEIR WEBS. MOST LINES OF SILK ARE ONLY 0.001 TO 0.004 MILLIMETER THICK.

There are many different types of spider silk. A single species of spider can make up to eight different types of silk, each one pulled through different spinnerets.

From Babies to Bungee Jumps

Some spider silk is tough and stretchy. This can be used as a bungee rope that the spider travels down, or it can be used to build the frame for a web. A stickier type of silk is used to fill in the web. This is what catches food for the spider to eat.

A softer type of silk is used to wrap up food and spider babies. Spider babies are called spiderlings.

A WORLD WITHOUT SPIDERS

A Webless World

If there were no spiders, there would be no webs, either. Of all the species of spiders, about half of them make webs to trap their food. There are many different types of webs. The most common is an orb web.

Orb Web

Net-Casting Spider

Some spiders make very strange-looking webs. The net-casting spider spins silk between its front legs and creates a net. It then hangs overhead, waiting for something to walk past so it can jump down and catch its dinner in the net.

Liquefied Insects

Before eating, spiders vomit juices on or into their **prey**. The juices turn creatures from solid to liquid – like turning food into drink. The spiders then suck up the soupy body parts and insides.

Out of 40,000 species of spiders, there's only one that eats plants. Every other type of spider only eats other creatures.

See You Later, Spiders

If all the spiders disappeared tomorrow, nobody knows what would happen for sure. Maybe humans would find a way to replace spiders and solve all the problems. But what if we couldn't? Throughout this book, we are going to take a look at what might happen in a world without spiders.

100 INSECTS AND COUNTING

An Insect's Worst Nightmare

Most spiders eat insects and they eat a lot of them. Although we don't always notice spiders, we would notice insects if spiders weren't there. Spiders eat around 2,000 insects a year. Houses would be crawling with insects if it weren't for spiders.

Circle of Life

Animals eaten by other animals are called prey. Animals that eat other animals are called predators. Spiders are both predators and prey. As long as predators like spiders are around, the number of insects will be controlled.

There are 27.5 million tons of spiders in the world. They are found on every continent except Antarctica.

Perfect Predators

Out of all the creatures that eat insects, spiders are probably the most important. This is because they are very, very good at it. Spiders are one of the top predators in the world, alongside humans. Altogether, spiders eat 440 million to 880 million tons of insects every year.

ALL THE HUMANS IN THE WORLD WEIGH AROUND 440-550 MILLION TONS.

THIS MEANS THAT IT WOULD ONLY TAKE AROUND A YEAR FOR SPIDERS TO EAT EVERY HUMAN ON THE PLANET!

BREAKING NEWS:

FOOD RUNNING OUT

BREAKING NEWS

Stores have now completely run out of some types of food, such as fruits, vegetables, and grains. This will affect other animals, too. Luckily there are plenty of Brussels sprouts left – apparently even the insects don't want them.

What Are Crops?

Crops are plants that are grown by humans in order to feed people. Farmers who look after crops worry about pests. A pest is any creature that eats or destroys crops. Most pests are insects. When spiders eat the insects, they keep our crops safe.

This pest is a type of insect called a locust.

Lots of food comes from crops. Just 12 crops make up three-quarters of the world's food. Rice, corn, and wheat are the most important three crops of all. Wheat is turned into flour, which is used when making things like bread and cake. Many fruits and vegetables are also grown by farmers.

Popcorn is made from corn. If there were no spiders, the insects would steal all of your popcorn.

MANY CROPS, SUCH AS CLOVER AND ALFALFA, ARE USED TO FEED FARM ANIMALS SUCH AS COWS.

Rise of the Pests

Without spiders, huge swarms of insects would overrun the fields. Insects have lots of babies, and their populations can get bigger very quickly. They would eat everything in their path before it has even been picked and sent to the stores.

LUNCH BOXES

AND GAS MASKS

These farmers are spraying pesticides on crops of rice.

The Human Way

Farmers have their own way to deal with pests. They use **chemicals** called pesticides. These can be dangerous to all sorts of insects and animals – even humans. Many crops are protected by a mixture of pesticides and spiders.

If there were no more spiders eating insects, farmers all over the world would need to use a lot more pesticides. Pesticides can already be found in the air, ground, and in lakes and other waters. Traces can sometimes be found on food sold in the stores, although not enough to be dangerous.

Pesticides might be breathed in, swallowed in water or food, or **absorbed** through the skin.

Chemicals Everywhere

However, if a lot more pesticide was being sprayed all over the world, these small traces could become a much bigger problem for humans. Humans who work with pesticides have to wear all sorts of equipment, such as **protective** clothing, goggles, and respirators.

Respirators are masks worn on the face that clean the air before it is breathed in. In the past, respirators were sometimes called gas masks.

ANOTHER

DOCTOR'S NOTE

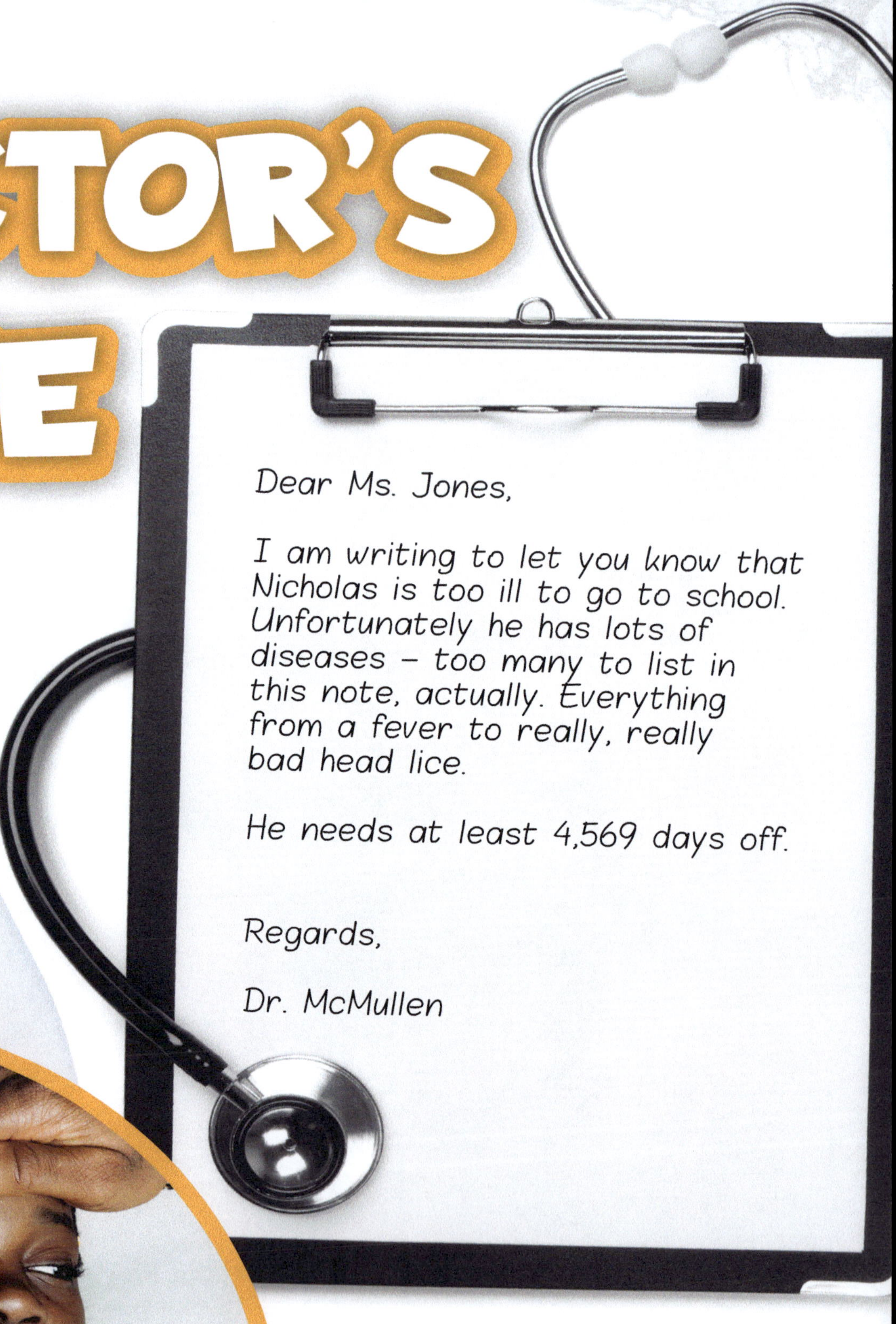
Dear Ms. Jones,

I am writing to let you know that Nicholas is too ill to go to school. Unfortunately he has lots of diseases – too many to list in this note, actually. Everything from a fever to really, really bad head lice.

He needs at least 4,569 days off.

Regards,

Dr. McMullen

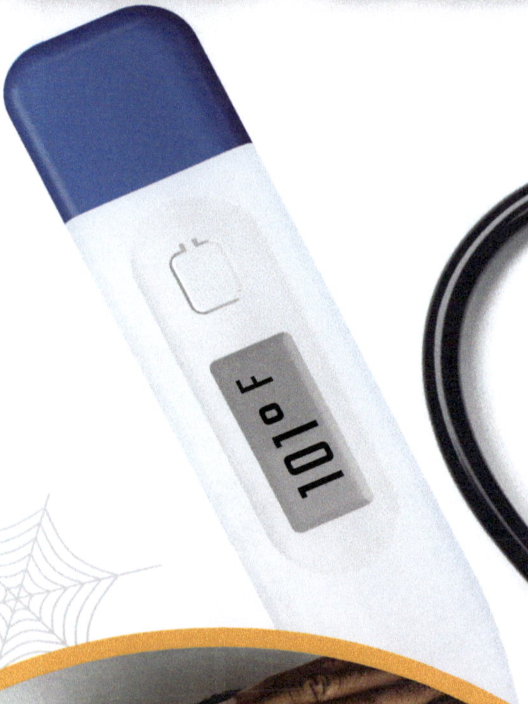

Disease

Many diseases are carried by insects. They usually spread their diseases to humans by biting them. Some diseases spread by insects are common and not too dangerous. However, some insect diseases can be very dangerous.

Malaria

Malaria is a very dangerous disease that is spread by an insect called a mosquito. If treated quickly, malaria can be cured. However, in some areas of the world without advanced **health care**, malaria can be deadly.

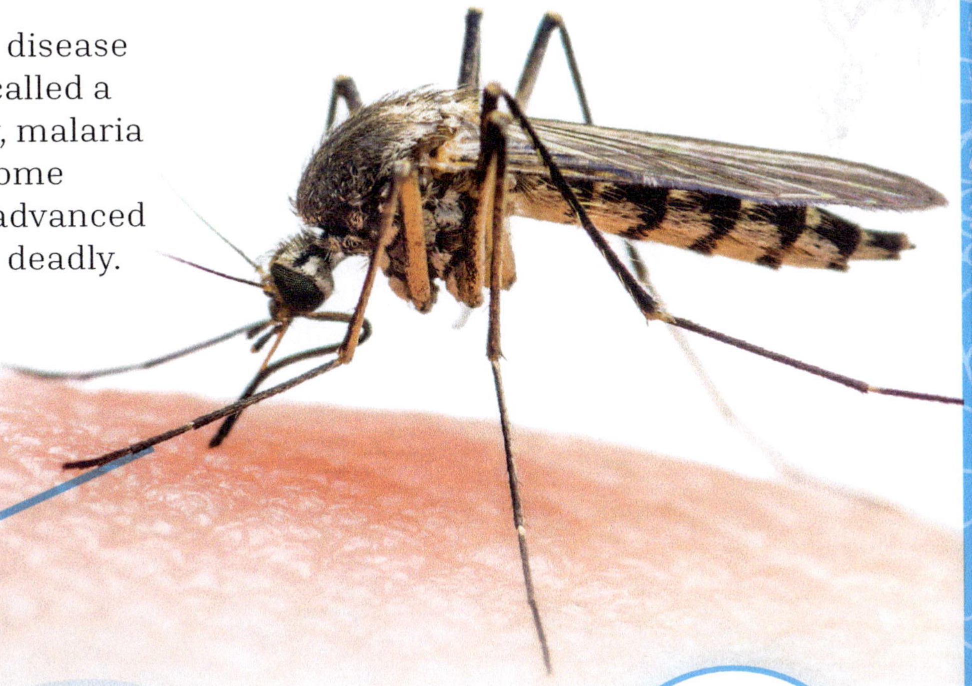

Mosquitoes, like this one, land on humans and suck their blood. This can spread malaria into the body.

IN 2014, THERE WERE 198 MILLION CASES OF MALARIA AROUND THE WORLD.

This jumping spider is eating a mosquito.

Although many people get infected with malaria, there would be many more cases if there were more mosquitos. Luckily, many mosquitoes are eaten by spiders. There are two species of jumping spiders that especially like eating mosquitoes. They will even ignore other insects in order to get their favorite food.

THE END OF SPIDER MILKING

Reporter: Welcome to the news at 6. We now have an interview with Mr. MacDonald. What was your job again?

MacDonald: Well, I USED to milk spiders, before they disappeared.

Reporter: Gross! Why?

MacDonald: I milked the spiders' fangs for venom.

Reporter: That's horrible! I don't want to know any more!

MacDonald: It's not horrible. You see, th-

Reporter: LA LA LA, I can't hear you!

Why Do People Milk Spiders for Venom?

Spider venom is used in some medicine. To milk spiders, a tiny electric shock is used. The shock causes the fangs to release venom, which is collected by the scientists.

Almost all spiders have venom. It is used to **paralyze** their prey. However, most spider venom is only dangerous to insects. There are only a few species that have venom powerful enough to affect humans.

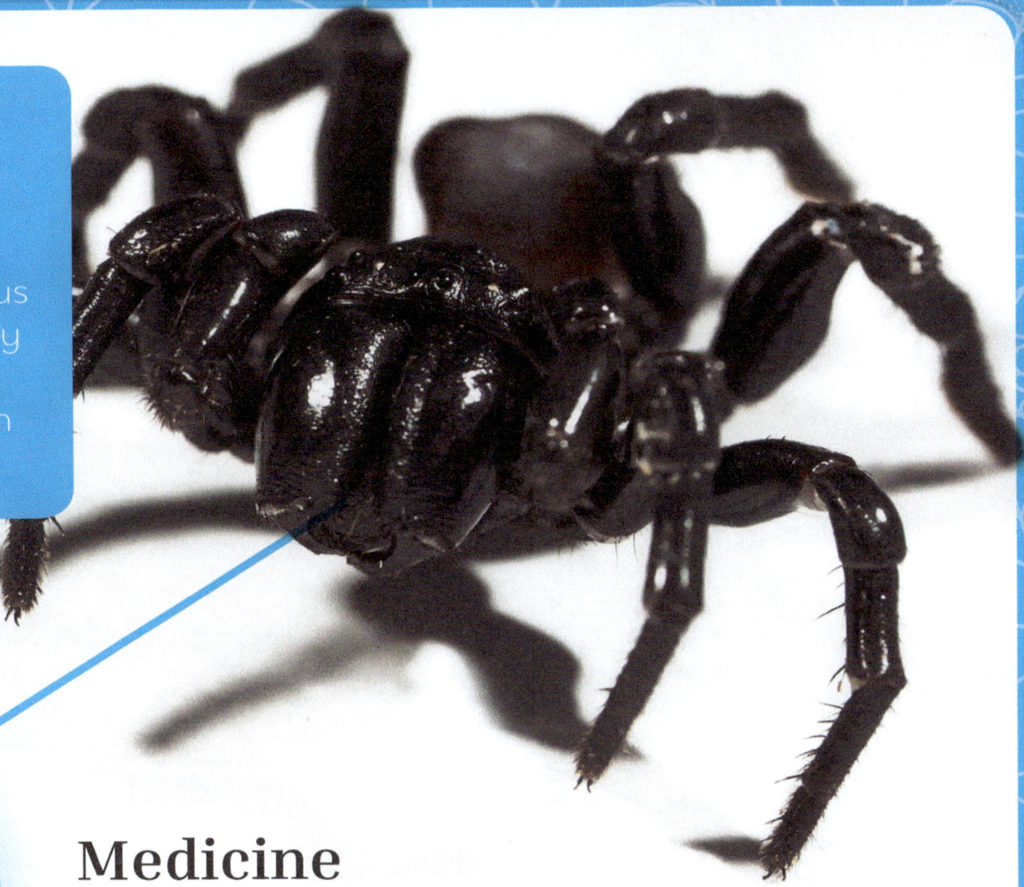

This is a funnel-web spider, one of the most dangerous in the world. They can be found in Australia, North America, and South America.

Medicine

Spider venom is used in medicine today, mainly in painkillers. Without spiders, we would have to find different ways to make some medicines. However, scientists think there are still new species that have not been found. New spider species could have venom that is able to make all sorts of new medicines.

Spider venom might also be used in the future to treat more serious diseases like **cancer** and **Alzheimer's disease.**

Spider Fangs

BULLETPROOF CLOTHES

The largest and strongest web is made by a spider called Darwin's bark spider. Its web can be 82 feet (25 m) wide.

Safe in Silk

Right now, research is being done to turn spider silk into protective things like bulletproof clothing. This might seem strange, but it is actually quite similar to how spiders use silk as well. A web is made to catch big insects flying very quickly. The silk needs to be tough and stretchy so it doesn't snap in half.

A bulletproof vest also wants to catch something flying very quickly – a bullet! A very small amount of silk is enough to catch a flying insect. If enough spider silk was put together, it would be a lot stronger. However, if spiders disappeared, nobody would have a chance to use their incredible silk.

How Many Spiders Would It Take?

Spiders tend to eat each other when put together. This means it is hard to get enough silk to create the clothing. For this reason, scientists hope to create a type of silkworm that could spin spider silk.

BRIDGE COLLAPSE

DAILY NEWS

World • Buisness • Finance • Lifestyle • Travel • Sports • Weather

TOWN BRIDGE DESTROYED BY STORM!

The old town bridge was destroyed last night. The materials it was made of were too weak to hold it up. Local scientist Dr. Amy Li said: "We were about to strengthen this bridge using spider silk. But we couldn't find any!"

This never would have happened if the spiders were here!

By D. Scase

After seeing the crumpled mess of rotted wood that was once a bridge, this reporter asked Dr. Li why the bridge wasn't strengthened sooner with steel or iron. "Oh, the mayor wouldn't allow that," she said. "He is obsessed with using spider-related materials." It seemed important to secure an interview with the arachnid-enamored enigma.

After gaining entrance to the mayor's office, this reporter managed to score a quick question-and-answer session with the man himself. "I just love spiders!" he said, eight times. With growing unease at his octuple outbursts – "I wish I was a spider! I wish I was a spider! I wish I was…" – this reporter made for the exit. A follow-up investigation is soon to come.

Other Uses for Spider Silk

Super-strong silk could have many uses for humans. For example, it could be used to strengthen airplanes, ships, and bridges.

Spider Goats

To make enough silk to be used, scientists might try to breed a type of goat that makes milk full of spider silk. Goats are bigger animals, and they would be able to create a lot more silk every day than a group of spiders.

Can It Be Stronger?

To make the spider silk even stronger, it could be mixed with other strong materials. Graphene (say: gra-feen) is an especially strong and light material made in **laboratories**. By feeding a little bit of this material to spiders, it made their silk even stronger than before.

IN THE FUTURE, SPIDER SILK MAY BE USED FOR SUTURES – THESE ARE ROWS OF STITCHES THAT DOCTORS USE TO REPAIR BIG CUTS.

Spider silk might be used in parachutes, too.

A DAY AT

THE ZOO

Spider Wasp

An Eight-Legged Dinner

Spiders are not just important because they eat insects – they are also important because they get eaten. Spiders are food for many animals all over the world. Some animals, such as spider wasps and the gold-tipped bat, eat nothing but spiders.

The Food Web

A food web is a **diagram** that shows which living things eat each other. A food web is usually made up of plants, plant-eating animals, and animal-eating animals. It shows us how all animals are connected. If one animal disappears, this can be bad for the whole web.

A Food Web

MORE THAN 8,000 SPECIES OF ANIMALS, INCLUDING MANY BIRDS, MAINLY EAT SPIDERS.

Breakfast for Birds

Spiders are an important food, especially for young birds. This is because spiders contain something called taurine. Taurine helps birds to grow up to be clever and brave. Without spiders, birds would have a less healthy diet. They might find it harder to survive.

Some birds catch lots of spiders to feed to their babies.

HISTORY

WITHOUT SPIDERS

Spider silk has been used for many things throughout history. If spiders had never existed, there would be many unexpected differences in today's world.

Seeing Stars

From the late 1800s to the 1960s, spider silk was used to make crosshairs in telescopes. A crosshair is used to help people look at things. Years ago, there was nothing as thin and as strong as spider silk. When **astronomers** tried looking into the night sky to see stars, the crosshairs would get in the way. However, thanks to spider silk, they were able to build better telescopes with thin, strong crosshairs.

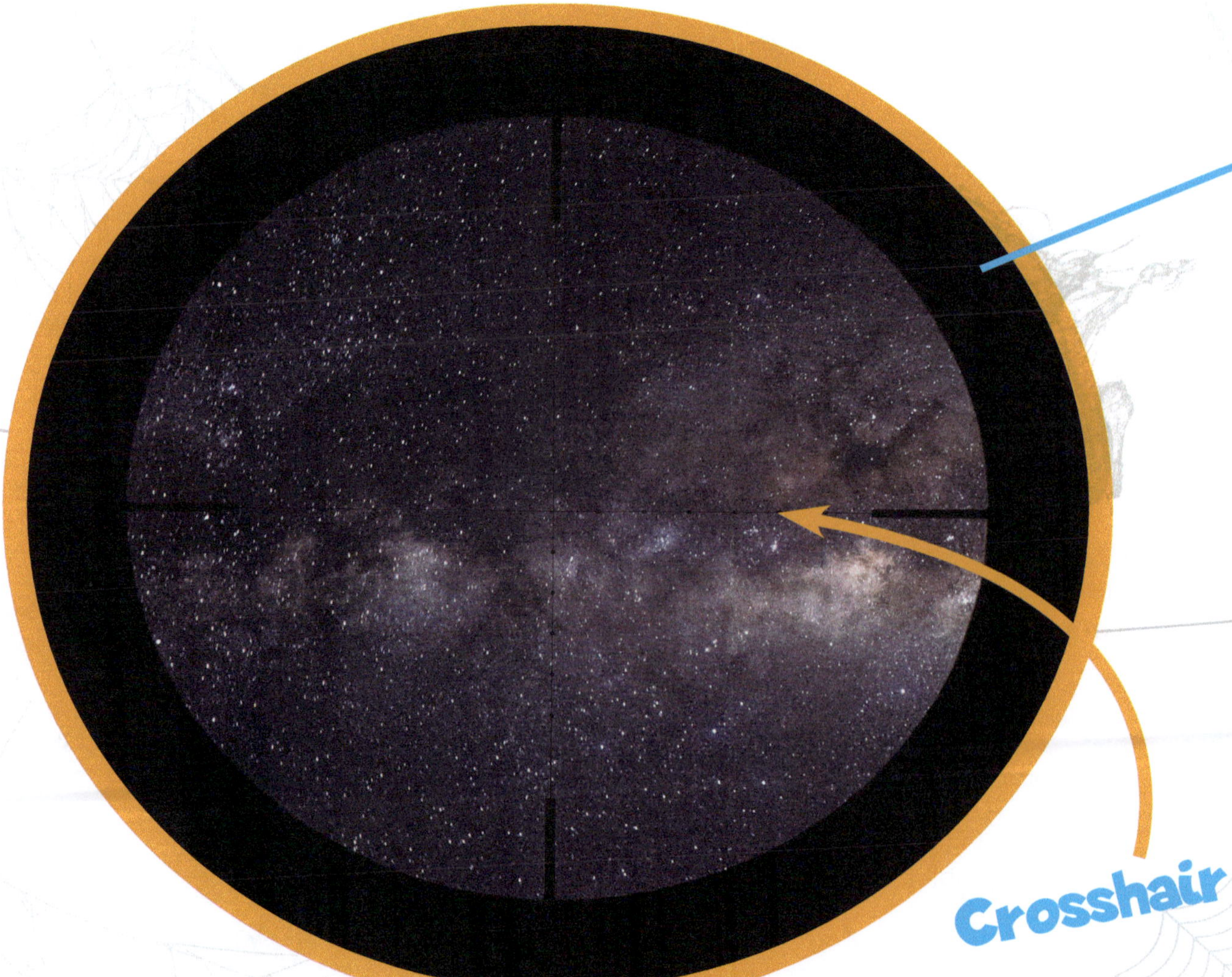

Winning Wars

In World War II, spider silk was used to make the crosshairs in guns. The thin silk was tough – even extreme temperatures and the guns' vibrations wouldn't break it. The silk crosshairs were encased in glass and would last for years.

Black widow spiders were often used when making the crosshairs.

Some spiders' silk can stretch up to three times its length before breaking.

Silk and Steel

Sometimes people say spider silk is stronger than steel. However, they should say that spider silk is tougher than steel. Silk is light, stretchy, and harder to break, whereas steel is heavy and can be bent out of shape. If you had a piece of spider silk that weighed the same as a piece of steel, the silk would be the toughest material.

THREATS

TO SPIDERS

These factories are burning an oil called petroleum. Petroleum is a **fossil fuel**.

A world without spiders looks scary. While we still have spiders in today's world, there are real threats to these creatures. If these threats become serious enough, there might be far fewer spiders in the future.

Climate Change

In order to power vehicles and to make energy, people burn fossil fuels. This releases a gas called carbon dioxide into the air. When the air contains more carbon dioxide, more heat is trapped on Earth. This leads to many problems, such as more extreme weather.

Climate Change and Habitats

A habitat is an animal's home. It has all the things that an animal needs to survive. However, climate change can change a habitat and make it hard for the animal to live. For example, some spiders do not catch as much food when it is raining. If a habitat changes and it rains all the time, the spiders in that area might die out.

Climate change can make a place hotter or colder. It can also change the amount of rainfall.

Humans sometimes destroy spider habitats by clearing away forests for farmland or building bigger cities.

When humans clear away forests to build things, it is called deforestation.

New Species

Sometimes humans bring new species into an area. This can cause many problems. For example, when a new species of ant was brought into Hawaii, they attacked the spiders that lived there and caused many problems.

Acid rain can be caused by climate change.

Acid Rain

When rain becomes too **acidic**, it can be harmful to all life, especially plants. In the Appalachian Mountains, acid rain can damage the spruce and fir trees. This destroys the habitat of the spruce-fir moss spider, which is an **endangered** spider.

Pesticides

Pesticides that are sprayed to kill insects can kill spiders, too. If too much pesticide is used, it might cause spiders to die out in certain areas. Chemicals from the pesticides can get into the **groundwater**, which is also bad for spiders.

Some pesticides are spread by airplanes.

Is There One Reason?

Spiders have a lot of things to deal with. There are lots of different reasons why spiders are threatened. Added up, these reasons create a real danger for spiders. However, there are things being done to save spiders and the rest of the environment.

SAVING THE SPIDERS

Although climate change is still a problem, humans have done many good things for the environment. For example, the Paris Climate Agreement is an agreement between countries to release less carbon dioxide into the air.

Wind Turbines

Solar Panels

THINGS LIKE SOLAR PANELS AND WIND TURBINES CREATE ELECTRICITY IN A WAY THAT IS FRIENDLY TO THE ENVIRONMENT. THIS IS CALLED GREEN ENERGY, AND IT IS MORE POPULAR THAN EVER.

What Can You Do to Help?

- Recycle! Ask an adult to help you find out what can be recycled.
- To save electricity, turn off things like lights and televisions when you are not using them. You could also ask your parents if they are using energy-saving light bulbs.
- Talk about spiders! Tell everyone that they are one of the most important tiny things in the world.

GLOSSARY

absorbed has taken in or soaked up

acidic contains a chemical substance that causes damage to the natural environment

Alzheimer's disease a disease that affects the brain and memory, usually when someone becomes old

astronomers people who study the universe and objects in space

cancer a serious disease caused by the uncontrolled dividing of cells

chemicals matter that can be mixed with other matter to cause changes

diagram a picture that makes something easier to understand

diverse full of things that are different from each other

endangered when a species of animal is in danger of going extinct

fossil fuel fuels, such as coal, oil, and gas, that formed millions of years ago from the remains of animals and plants

glands organs in the body that produce chemical substances for the body to use or get rid of

groundwater the water found among dirt and rock underground

health care a system set up by a country so that people are looked after if they get ill

laboratories rooms or buildings that have the technology needed to perform scientific experiments

paralyze to make something unable to move

prey animals that are hunted by other animals for food

protective a thing that keeps someone or something safe

span the full length of something from end to end

INDEX